MW01640118

MEOW!

Louis Weber, CEO
Publications International, Ltd.
7373 North Cicero Avenue
Lincolnwood, Illinois 60712

www.pilbooks.com

Manufactured in China.

8 7 6 5 4 3 2 1

ISBN: 978-1-4508-9991-8

WORLD OF CRANKY CATS

new seasons®

It's just what happens when
you go to St. Maarten without me.

One down,
two to go.

You may sit on the couch
only with my permission.

BATH is a four-letter word....

And she calls me a bitch?

Does this scarf
make my head look FAT?

MINE!

Any questions?

I don't purr.

It's funny how you think
I'm listening to you....

Don't even think about it.

What do you mean,
cats can't have Botox?

My. Toys.
Not. Yours.

Who *says* opposites attract?

Who you callin' fat?

I'm not being lazy. I'm reducing my carbon footprint.

I had fun once.
It was awful.

If each day is a gift,
I'd like to know where
I can return Mondays....

I SAID I have a HEADACHE!

Talk to me after
I've had my coffee.

Is THAT what you're wearing?

Did you forget I have allergies?

Can you hear me now?

Guess who decided not
to use the litterbox today!

Now I understand
why we have a dog....

I hate housework.

Who is Aunt Karen, and why does she need a scarf anyway?

Indoor cat, I am an INDOOR cat!

Every cat deserves
two fur coats in her life.

What's the password?

Yes, I have been told I look like a snowy owl before. Thanks.

Keeping calm and carrying on.

Always a bridesmaid ...
never a bride.

Here's lookin' at you, jerk.

Don't even get me started.

I'm having a bad whisker day....

What does a guy have to do to get a drink around here?

With special thanks to:
Jennifer Barney, Karen Hartman, Anne O'Connor,
Frank Putrino, Anita Remijas, Barbara Rittenhouse, Mimi Roeder,
Kathleen Rose, Helene Shapiro, Patty Sprague, Linda Weber, Leslie Weyhrich

Additional photography: Shutterstock.com